CHECK LIST FOR
A PERFECT WEDDING

CHECK LIST FOR
A PERFECT WEDDING

REVISED EDITION

BY

BARBARA LEE FOLLETT

Dolphin Books
Doubleday & Company, Inc.
Garden City, New York

Dolphin Books Original edition: 1961

Revised editions: 1967, 1973

ISBN: 0-385-04251-5
Library of Congress Catalog Card Number 72–97272
Copyright © 1961, 1967, 1973
by Barbara Lee Follett and Robert de Roos
All Rights Reserved
Printed in the United States of America

TO MY FAMILY

TERI
the delightful bride

BEN
the generous father of the bride

LEE
the helpful and encouraging son
(and occasional comedy relief)

MOTHER AND FATHER
always an inspiration

CONTENTS

INTRODUCTION

Congratulations and best wishes!

You are engaged. The groom's parents have called on your parents. Family and close friends have been told the good news. Proper announcements of the engagement have been sent to the newspapers. Now the hectic fun of planning the wedding is before you. This book takes over to help you.

Wedding plans equal lists, and lists equal efficiency. In this check list you will find the perfect formula for your perfect wedding. It is correct, complete and in chronological order.

First, look over the book to see what lies before you. Are you overwhelmed? Ready to elope? Wait! Just follow the items of instruction one by one as they are listed. When each item has been taken care of *to fit your personal taste and pocketbook*—or if an item does not apply to your plan—*check it off and forget it*. When all the items have been attended to, you will have a perfect wedding with a minimum of confusion.

While this check list is addressed to happy brides-to-be the world over, it is designed equally for the mother of the bride. Sometimes it is difficult to tell where the bride's tasks end and the mother of the bride takes over.

My own role was that of mother of the bride, and I found that while the bride blissfully and rightfully floated along on her personal cloud, many of the more earthy tasks fell to me. We have all attended many weddings, but we tend to overlook the details. That is as it should be: The machinery never shows in a carefully planned wedding, but it is always there.

How many mothers of brides-to-be have awakened in the middle of the night startled by unanswered questions? "I don't know the clergyman. Am I supposed to invite him? If so, do I invite his wife?" Or, "How can I cope with both Ted's mother and his stepmother?" Or, "Is the caterer furnishing the ice, or should I order it?" "What is Sue supposed to do with six toasters?"

Having found the answers to these questions and every other question that needed answering, I noted them.

My own check list was saved at the request of many friends who sensed that the serenity of our daughter's wedding could have resulted only from careful planning. Many other brides and their mothers have since used this list. They have found that the days leading up to the wedding and the wedding day itself were simplified—therefore more enjoyable —because of it. In passing on this tested information* to you, I hope you will use it with confidence and pleasure.

A note to the bride-to-be: It is *your* wedding. Certain customs are traditional. Other details can be arranged to suit you. You want a happy, serene and memorable day—not a stage production. The elaborateness or cost of your wedding will not be the factor that will make it outstanding, so do not put a financial strain on your parents or yourself. Feel free to eliminate expensive frills. The wedding should be keyed to your own desires and finances—not to the groom's financial status. But *do not economize on effort and planning*— the essentials that will make your wedding beautiful and add to your guests' enjoyment and comfort.

If you have been married before, a simple gathering of family and close friends is your best choice—especially if you have been divorced. A white wedding gown is traditional dress for a first marriage—not a second. At a second wedding, there is usually only one attendant to serve as a witness. Most newspapers will announce a second marriage, but not a second engagement. If it is your husband's second marriage but

---

* Editor's note: Mrs. Follett referred originally to her CHECK LIST having been tested by many of her friends. It has now been tested and enthusiastically approved as a wedding essential by hundreds of thousands of users.

your first, plan any kind of wedding which pleases both of you.

Preparing for your wedding can be tiring. I give you these words of caution: Save your energy; limit the number of parties and showers; because your bridesmaids are included in most parties, do not let showers become a financial burden to them. Special note: Showers are never given by close relatives of the bride or groom.

Weddings can be fun, especially if your nerves are not frayed by too many details. Go to sleep each night with the assurance that when you awaken next day, you have only to consult your check list. It will do the worrying for you. Relax. Enjoy the excitement and have fun.

BARBARA LEE FOLLETT
(MRS. BENJAMIN FOLLETT)

THE RIGHT START

Several things are essential in planning a wedding. First is this check list. Second is a file-card system. Sound complicated? Do not be frightened. It is quite simple and absolutely indispensable. Third is a calendar. There is one in the back of this book. Fourth is a notebook in which to list gifts as they arrive.

Get plenty of three-by-five filing cards and a file box with alphabetical dividers. Now start on the guest list. Your list will start with your own family and friends. Your father may want to include some business friends. The groom and his parents will add their lists. Make out an individual filing card for each prospective guest. Example:

> CARTER, Mr. and Mrs. John
> 810 Fifth Avenue
> San Francisco
> California 94406

File the cards alphabetically. Keep going over the cards, and *think* as you go. You will remember that Mr. and Mrs. Carter have a daughter who is over sixteen. She should receive a separate invitation (do not economize on this), so type a card for her too. The bridesmaids may have brothers and sisters and parents to be invited individually (never put "and family" on the invitations) and their cards will go into the correct place in the file box.

After the various lists have been transferred to cards and filed, you may find duplications you might have missed otherwise. The flexibility of the file system will save you from copying lists endlessly. When you have decided on the final guest list, mark the corners of the cards "church only," "reception only," "announcement only," or whatever meets your wishes.

After using the cards to address the invitations (check each card as the invitation is addressed), make an alphabetical master list, using only last names. (I taped my list to the back of a door.) This is your check list for noting responses. As the responses come in, note the *number* of people accepting—for example: Carter: 2. This will make it easy to arrive at the final total. Cross off the names of people who send regrets. If you type your list, make a carbon for the groom and his family. They will appreciate it.

Have a divider in your file box labeled "Services," for the names, addresses, and phone numbers of the florist, caterer, photographer, and so on.

When a gift arrives, list it by number in your gift register. Tape a duplicate number to the gift. Be sure to record the name of the store in the register. This will be a help in checking errors and is indispensable when gifts have to be returned. (Exchanges are permissible, but a little tact and discretion are indicated.) It is helpful to save the boxes of gifts you know will have to be returned.

When you check your file card for the address of the donor to write your thank-you letter, record the gift on the file card. This will give you a quick reference and will help you meet many a diplomatic crisis. A flip of the file will instantly remind you of the treasure Great-aunt Acanthus sent.

Keep up with your thank-you notes—otherwise they can become a burden instead of a pleasure. If the gift is from Mr. and Mrs. Giftsender, address your thanks to them both. Include your fiancé's name in the body of the letter ("Bob and I will love the beautiful glasses . . ."), but sign only your own name. Use unadorned paper or your own monogram. It is too soon to use the groom's initials.

A sharp warning: some brides have the mistaken idea that their busy schedule excuses them from writing prompt thank-you notes. This myth has been the cause of many misunderstandings and consequent bitter criticism of the bride and her family. Think of the time, effort, and money your friends spent on you. They have every right to expect a prompt, warm, personal letter in return.

The groom's mother will appreciate having a list of gifts and donors so she will know what gifts her friends sent. If the bride-to-be is away from home, she will need a carbon copy so she can get to her thank-you notes. If she is going on a long honeymoon or is moving to another city, it is wise to list which gifts are to be stored, exchanged, or shipped. These notes may be made in the gift register.

A reminder: The bride should not give information to the newspapers about parties given in her honor without her hostess' permission.

Two items included with malice aforethought:

1. Many people of experience advise against including a flower girl or ring bearer in the wedding party. Children are notorious scene stealers. If you want to risk scene stealing on your big day, see page 71.

2. Consider the hazards of house guests. The best-meaning relatives and friends can be very wearing when you are busy and need to conserve your energy. Guests expect to be entertained, they are usually starving, and they may drain away all the hot water in the house at a critical moment.

If friends offer to house your guests, accept gratefully. Another solution is to reserve rooms for your out-of-town guests at the same hotel or motel to make your transportation tasks simpler.

THE ESSENTIAL PRELIMINARIES

Allow as much time as you can for these first steps. Every step you take early does not have to be taken later—in the days when showers and parties abound. From now on, simply follow this check list. As you complete these items and record the relevant data, *check off* the instructions and forget them.

1. Decide what type of wedding you will have, the degree of formality and approximate size.

2. Set the date and hour for the wedding. Reserve the church and make certain the clergyman is available. At the same time, reserve the church for rehearsal (see page 19). Note the correct full name of the church for invitations.

3. With your groom, arrange a time to meet your clergyman for a personal talk. Make a calendar note.

4. Set a time to talk to your clergyman or his secretary about the details of the wedding and the rehearsal (see page 19). Make a calendar note.

5. After considering the size of your guest list, decide where you will hold the reception. Note: Experience shows that from one fourth to one third of those invited will be unable to attend.

6. Select the bridesmaids from among your close friends. Don't choose your maid or matron of honor "from the ranks." Invite her specifically for this special place. If the groom has a sister of reasonable age, invite her to be a bridesmaid. This can be the first step toward a good relationship.

7. Remind the groom to select his ushers and best man and hope he will include your brother. One usher is needed for every fifty guests. There need not be the same number of bridesmaids as ushers.

8. Copy bridesmaids' and ushers' names and addresses on your file cards; you will need them frequently. Make up duplicate lists of bridesmaids and ushers for friends who will want to include them in pre-wedding parties.

6

9. Notify newspapers in writing of the names in the wedding party.

10. Begin the card file of wedding guests. Ask the groom and his family to send in their lists of guests. Designate the number of guests you can accommodate. The groom's family does not always realize how early you will need their lists, SO SET A DEADLINE.

11. If the reception is to be held at your home, begin now to plan for the garden, house décor, cleaning of house before the reception (use blank pages for your notes).

12. If the reception is to be held at a hotel, restaurant or club, make the reservation now.

13. Engage caterer. Note his name and phone number in the file system under "Services." Note date of appointment to discuss details—at least two weeks before the wedding and preferably sooner (see page 26).

14. Engage photographer. Note his name and telephone number on a file card under "Services." Set a date for a conference—either by telephone or in person—at least three weeks before the wedding. Make a calendar note (see page 31).

15. Engage florist. Note his name and telephone on a file card under "Services." Set a date for a conference as early as possible, but no later than three weeks before the wedding. Make a calendar note (see page 29).

16. Arrange for music at the church. Note: Some churches provide the organist and will not permit outside musicians. Ask the fee and arrange for payment before or after the wedding day. Note name in file (see page 33).

17. Engage musicians for the reception. Note name in your file under "Services." Set a date for a conference for selection of music. Make a calendar note. Arrange for billing either before or after the reception (see page 34).

7

18. Hire limousines or arrange with friends to take the wedding party to and from the church. Be certain to arrange transportation from the church for the groom's parents so they can reach the reception promptly. Note names and telephone numbers under "Services." Arrange for billing either before or after the wedding day (see page 35).

19. Shop for wedding gown and veil. If gown has to be ordered, allow at least six weeks for delivery (see page 21).

20. Shop for mother-of-the-bride's dress. It is sometimes difficult to find the right dress and accessories.

21. Buy wedding shoes and lingerie before the fitting of the wedding gown. And break in those shoes!

22. Order note paper for your thank-you letters. If you have it monogrammed, use your own initials, but don't overbuy.

23. Select bridesmaids' dresses and headpieces. The choice of these outfits is up to the bride. Discuss a satisfactory price range with the bridesmaids. They pay for their own outfits (see page 24).

24. Notify attendants to go to store for measurements and to order dresses.

25. Remind everyone (bride, groom and his family, and anyone else) that the deadline for the invitation list is nearing.

26. The bride and groom should select silver, china, crystal, and linen patterns. (For monogramming, see page 46). List the stores in your file. Friends will often ask where you are listed, bless their hearts!

27. Shop for your going-away outfit and trousseau. Make a schedule. Select a going-away costume that will serve you well for a year at least (see page 22).

28. Set a date for house or apartment-hunting. Set dates for shopping for furniture. Make a calendar note.

29. Check on the bridesmaids. Have they ordered their dresses?

30. Order wedding invitations as soon as you have settled on the number of guests. Order a few extra; some will be spoiled in addressing (see page 37).

31. While you are at the stationery store, order the bride's stationery trousseau: Calling cards, informals and formal notes, everyday paper (see page 45).

32. Meet bridesmaids to shop for shoes. Have them all dyed in one dye lot. Buy gloves if they are to be worn. Gloves may be a gift from the bride (see page 24).

33. Select proper shade of stockings for bridesmaids and have each girl buy a pair. Order another pair for emergencies. Have stockings delivered with the dresses.

34. Buy a lipstick and nail polish for all attendants to use. That way, all will wear the same shade.

35. When bridesmaids' dresses arrive at the store, notify the attendants to appear for fittings. Instruct fitter to co-ordinate proper dress length for all attendants (see page 25).

36. Have the invitations arrived? Perhaps you had better check. See page 37 for addressing instructions.

37. When the mother of the bride has selected her outfit, describe it to the groom's mother: length of dress, length of sleeves, color, and degree of formality. To create a harmonious picture in the receiving line, colors and styles must be co-ordinated. It is customary for the bride or her mother to suggest a selection of colors for the groom's mother to choose from. Black clothing is specifically banned. Weddings, while solemn, should not be gloomy.

9

At a small home wedding: 1. The mothers need not wear hats or gloves. 2. If the wedding is limited to family and close friends, the mothers need not buy new dresses but may wear whatever is suitable for the time of day. 3. If a judge instead of a clergyman performs the ceremony, suggest he wear his judicial robes for added solemnity.

THE FOUR WEEKS BEFORE THE WEDDING

The tempo begins to quicken. There are just four more weeks before your wedding day. No reason for panic—just take one step at a time and all will be done.

38. Mail invitations. Have master list of guests' names ready to check off the number of people accepting. Early invitations mean early responses and early arrival of gifts—and more time for the bride's important thank-you notes. Reread page 2.

39. Arrange for fitting of the bride's gown. Make a calendar note.

40. If your calendar is filling with parties, you might like to send a schedule to your bridesmaids.

41. Make an appointment with your doctor for a complete physical checkup. Note date on calendar. If a blood test is required in your state, have it done at the same time as the physical.

42. Remind the groom to get his blood test.

43. Make an appointment with your dentist for a checkup and any necessary work. Make a calendar note.

44. Select groom's ring, if it is to be a double-ring ceremony, and have it engraved. This might be the time to select a gift for him. (This is optional.)

11

45. Select gifts for bridesmaids. Suitable gifts: earrings, a charm, any small piece of jewelry, a picture frame, a compact. It is nice to engrave the gift with the wedding date and the recipient's initials. A more expensive version of the bridesmaids' gift may be given to your maid or matron of honor.

46. Remind the groom to select gifts for his ushers. These gifts should also be of the "keepsake" type.

47. Set up a table for gift display. If the reception is to be held at home, you will want them well displayed. In any event, you will want to have close friends in to see your gifts (see page 52).

48. Check your luggage. Do you have enough for your honeymoon? Put it in your room so preliminary packing can begin.

49. To relieve any possible tendency to snap, how about a small champagne-testing party now?

50. Obtain a floater policy to cover the wedding gifts.

51. Change Social Security card to married name.

52. Change bride's name on insurance policies. Remind groom to change the beneficiary on his life-insurance policies.

53. Make out a will.

54. Change bride's name on her driver's license.

55. Make an appointment for hair and manicure early in the week of the wedding. Note time on calendar. Try to avoid that "just-out-of-the-beauty-shop" look.

56. Open a bank account in new name.

57. Order thank-you gifts for hostesses who entertain for the bride. (Write thank-you notes the day after each party.)

58. Write to society editors of newspapers and request their wedding forms. Most editors want these forms completed about ten days in advance of the wedding. Remember out-of-town papers. List the papers: The photographer will want them.

59. Plan housing arrangements for out-of-town attendants. This is your responsibility.

60. Think ahead to the time right after the wedding reception (see page 78). There may be out-of-town guests to be entertained. Make your plans now.

61. Will you need a policeman or other attendant to direct parking at the reception? Engage him now and arrange to be billed either before or after the wedding day.

62. Keep up with your thank-you notes.

63. Arrange for someone to help the bride dress on the day of the wedding. Set a time for her to be at your home. List on a file card.

64. If you want to be really extravagant, have your hairdresser come to your home to comb your hair, and the bridesmaids' too. It is a delightful luxury.

65. Invite the clergyman. The mother of the bride *personally* gives the clergyman an engraved invitation addressed to him and his wife.

66. Get marriage license. Note a convenient time on the calendar.

67. Arrange spinster dinner or luncheon—perhaps on the same night as the bachelor dinner. Only your attendants need be present. This is an opportune time to give them their gifts and show them your trousseau and gifts.

13

68. Save some of the ribbons from your gift packages. Let your bridesmaids make them into a mock bouquet to use at the wedding rehearsal.

69. A rehearsal party is given before or after the rehearsal, frequently the night before the wedding. Do not stay out too late. Invite husbands and wives or fiancés of the wedding party. It is a nice gesture for the groom's family to give this party, but it may be given by anyone, including the bride's family—away from home, for sanity's sake.

70. Address and stamp announcements. They must be mailed *after* the wedding. Give them to a trustworthy friend to mail the day after the wedding. Then you can forget this detail.

71. Arrange for an attendant or a friend to stay in the room where gifts are displayed. She may help keep ash trays cleared and be generally helpful.

72. Arrange a place for the bridesmaids to dress. This will avoid confusion on the day of the wedding when you want things to run smoothly. Tell attendants what time you want them at your home for photographs and to be driven to the church.

73. Send reserved-pew cards or tell special guests and family members where they are to sit (see page 50).

74. Make sure the head usher understands about the reserved pews and passes the information along to the other ushers. Relatives can become very upset if this is neglected.

75. Give each usher a card with the names and numbers of the special pew holders, in case guests leave their cards at home.

14

76. Select a responsible person to handle the guest book at the reception. This may be a youthful relative or a close friend who just missed being a bridesmaid. She may be stationed ahead of the receiving line, but not too close. Lay out two pens with the guest book when the time comes.

77. You have probably thought of it a hundred times, but because this list tries to include everything, remember that you will need: 1. something old; 2. something new; 3. something borrowed; 4. something blue.

78. Last reminder: Check the caterer, florist, photographer, musicians, hired drivers. Check the delivery date of the wedding gown, the church arrangements, and the cakemaker. A phone call to each can assure you all is in order.

THE LAST WEEK

Plan to slow down this week. If you have kept up faithfully with your thank-you notes, here is your reward: You may now relax with a clear conscience. Now aren't you glad you wrote all those notes?

79. Gather in one place everything you will need to dress for the wedding: gown, veil, underthings, stockings, cosmetics. Think. Then put everything together. Let there be no last-minute rushing about for stockings or a jar of cosmetics, or a last-gasp discovery that something you need has been packed.

80. Count acceptances for the reception and estimate the number of late responders. Notify the caterer. A few people will always bring uninvited children or friends. Prayer is the only defense against this.

81. Arrange for the best man to drive the getaway car or order a car or taxi. Arrange for best man to hide the honeymoon car or take care of train or plane reservations. If the bride and groom are to stay at a local hotel, *pre-register* them at the hotel of their choice.

82. Remind maid of honor that it is her duty to inform the bride's parents and the groom's parents when the bride and groom are ready to leave after the reception. This is to allow a moment for good-bys.

83. Pack suitcases for the honeymoon. Lay out everything to be packed and check and recheck. Put honeymoon luggage in the honeymoon car the night before the wedding.

84. Arrange your going-away handbag well ahead of time, while you are still thinking clearly.

85. You and your mother should read and reread the guest list to familiarize yourselves with the names. It will help when the receiving line forms.

86. Whoops! Let's not forget Father. He wants to look his best. Remind him to have his suit fitted and get everything ready for the big day. Give him some help.

87. Arrange for a supply of sandwiches or snacks for the wedding party, photographers, dressers, and others who will be in your home on the wedding day.

88. If you are in doubt about how long it will take you to dress, have a "dress rehearsal" so there will be no rush on the wedding day.

89. Make up a little emergency kit—safety pins, bobby pins, facial tissue—for someone to take to the church.

90. Most important: Make out a time chart for the wedding day and tape it to your mirror. *Allow extra time all down the line*. If everything is done in *slow motion*, you will find the *appearance of calmness* actually will make you *feel calm*.

91. Give your maid of honor the lipstick and nail polish attendants plan to use.

92. Have a box of clean tissue paper ready for the ride to the church. Place the tissue under and around the bride's gown to keep it from mussing. Note to bride: do not sit on your dress. Carefully place the train on the back of the car seat.

93. Board Fido and Puss and all other livestock on the day of the wedding. They do not belong.

94. It is the day of the wedding! It is a glorious day. Simply follow your time schedule. Bathe slowly. Someone is coming to help you with your dress and veil. Everything is together and ready.

95. Take care with your make-up, which must last for several hours. Test lipstick. Apply it "permanently"; blot and powder between applications. Use an effective anti-perspirant or deodorant.

96. Use a light touch with your make-up. Do not try anything dramatically startling today.

97. Wear little or no jewelry with your wedding gown. Jewelry might detract from your own beauty—and every bride is beautiful.

98. You have taken care of all the details. There is nothing to be concerned about. Forget the mechanics now and make this a perfect day. Enjoy every moment and savor each one for the years to come. Happy wedding!

CHURCH ARRANGEMENTS

Name of clergyman_____Phone_____

Full and correct name of church_____

_____

Address_____Phone_____

Clergyman's secretary_____Phone_____

SET UP AN APPOINTMENT TO DISCUSS THE WEDDING

1. Rules regarding photography inside the church.

2. Decorations. Any restrictions on flowers? Candles.

3. Facilities for the bridal party.

4. Does the church provide a kneeling cushion?

5. Is it necessary to have permission to be married in case of divorce or marriages of mixed religion? Are marriages permitted on Sunday? During Lent? Any restriction regarding bridesmaids', best man's or ushers' religion?

6. Payment for sexton.

7. Permission from the clergyman or his secretary for soloists, choir, other music or guest-singing participation.

8. Approval for special vows you may wish to incorporate.

9. If you and your husband-to-be are of different faiths, you may want to inquire if a clergyman representing each of your faiths may officiate jointly.

TIME FOR REHEARSAL—

WEDDING GOWN AND VEIL

NOTES:

FINAL SELECTION

Store_____Phone_____

Salesperson_____Extension_____

Fitting appointment_____

Remember to buy the wedding shoes and underthings before the fitting. Remember to break in the shoes.

Gloves: If your gown has long sleeves, there is no need for gloves. With a shorter-sleeved dress consider: 1. Short gloves a half-size larger than you usually wear—so you can slip off the left glove and give it to the maid-of-honor to hold. 2. Fingerless mitts. 3. If you wear long gloves, have the store unsew the seams of the ring finger. You will wear your engagement ring on your right hand on the day of the wedding. This is so that the wedding ring may properly be placed first on your finger.

At a small home wedding: 1. Gloves are inappropriate. 2. You may wear a long dress if you care to. 3. A short white dress, with or without a veil, is appropriate. 4. If the wedding is limited to family and close friends, you may prefer to be married in your going-away suit without a veil.

TROUSSEAU

The selection of your trousseau is a highly individual matter, but here are a few tips.

Your going-away outfit should be a suit or a costume which will be the mainstay of your wardrobe for at least a year. Choose your accessories with this in mind.

Be realistic in selecting clothing which will fit into your new life.

It is considered wise to have enough clothing in your trousseau so you will not have to buy anything for about a year. Some parents, rather than have their daughters stock up for a full year, allow her a "credit" for a new dress or two or a coat during the year.

Go over your clothes carefully to see that they are in good condition. Check buttons and snaps, the heels of your shoes. Have everything spotlessly clean.

If you use nylon or other synthetics for your lingerie, do not overbuy. They last a long time and launder quickly.

Make a list of what is required to fill out your wardrobe.

CHECK THESE	ON HAND	NEEDED
Slips		
Bras		
Girdles		
Nighties		
Hostess outfits		
Shoes		
Hose		
Panties		
Coats		
Suits		
Dresses		
Gloves		
Handbags		
Hats		
Belts		

BRIDESMAIDS' GOWNS

When selecting your bridesmaids' dresses, consider your own color preference and the style, but also be certain to visualize the dresses in your church and reception settings. For example, pastels might look charming in a light and airy church, while stronger jewel tones would complement cathedral architecture. When in doubt, take a sample and judge it in its setting.

FINAL SELECTION

Store_____Phone_____

Salesperson_____Extension_____

BRIDESMAID_____BRIDESMAID_____

Size stockings_____Size stockings_____

Size dress_____Size dress_____

Size gloves_____Size gloves_____

BRIDESMAID_____	BRIDESMAID_____
Size stockings_____	Size stockings_____
Size dress_____	Size dress_____
Size gloves_____	Size gloves_____
BRIDESMAID_____	BRIDESMAID_____
Size stockings_____	Size stockings_____
Size dress_____	Size dress_____
Size gloves_____	Size gloves_____

1. If there is to be a "junior" bridesmaid or flower girl, select a harmonizing dress, suitable for her age.

2. Tell the fitter to correlate the lengths of the bridesmaids' dresses.

3. Take a dress sample when you purchase lipsticks and nail polish.

4. Select proper stocking color.

5. Jewelry: Preferably, bridesmaids should not wear watches or bracelets. Simple earrings are enough.

NOTE: To avoid misunderstandings, type a list of instructions for the wedding week and deliver one to each bridesmaid with her dyed shoes.

1. Break in the new shoes.
2. List the party schedule.
3. Time and place for the rehearsal.
4. Time and place for the rehearsal dinner.
5. Place bridesmaids will dress for the wedding.
6. Time and place for the pre-wedding photographs.
7. Pairing with ushers for the drive from the wedding to the reception.

CATERER

Name_____ Phone_____

Address_____

Whether or not there is a caterer depends on you. "Catering" might mean only the hiring of extra help or the co-operation of kind friends. The time of day, the customs in your locality, the size of the wedding, the degree of formality, and the expense are the factors to be considered in planning the menu and the elaborateness of the service. Your own desires govern.

If your reception is to be held at a club or hotel, certain of the following items, such as glassware and dishes, will be taken care of automatically.

ITEMS TO BE CHECKED

1. Will the caterer furnish the wedding cake? If not, shop around; prices and workmanship vary considerably. In addition to the kind of cake, size, and cost, discuss:

A. Alternate decorations, instead of the little bride-and-groom figures so often seen atop cakes, can be flowers or wedding bells made of icing. Better still are real flowers in a tiny glass set into the top of the cake.

B. It is exciting to have fruitcake for the topmost tier. This small cake can be put away to enjoy on your first anniversary.

C. Boxed wedding cake (to take home to dream on) is an unexpected and unnecessary luxury today.

2. You will need extra help. (Splurge this once.) Does the caterer provide the extra help? If the reception is not to be catered, friends and relatives will be glad to lend a hand.

3. Napkins. Do you want them printed with the bride's and groom's names or initials?

4. Match booklets. Do you want them printed with the names or initials?

5. Coat racks, if needed. If so, you'll need coat hangers too.

6. Chairs.

7. Glasses.

8. Dishes.

9. Punch bowl.

10. Silver.

11. Menu. Is there to be a formal, seated bride's table? Read reception notes on page 58.

12. Beverages.

13. Tubs to ice champagne.

14. Serving centers must be located.

15. Location of wedding-cake table.

16. Stationing of help—at front door to take wraps; to pass refreshments. If there is likely to be a long wait before guests can reach the receiving line, you might consider serving champagne while guests are waiting. Remember to place a table so guests can leave their glasses before greeting the bride and groom.

17. Rice, confetti, or rose petals to be passed before couple leaves.

18. Ice.

19. Cigarettes.

20. Ash trays.

21. Who will move the furniture before and after the reception?

22. Request caterer to place a box lunch in the getaway car. Include sandwiches and champagne and glasses. Make it festive.

23. Alternate plan in case of rain.

24. Some caterers offer the services of a hostess, who can be of great service in keeping the guests comfortable, telling

them when the cake is to be cut, the bouquet to be thrown, and so on. Well worth the money for a large reception.

25. Caterers are experienced in what they call "circulation" for serving, and in reception-line procedure. If you have a caterer, discuss your reception with him in detail. He may be able to suggest a previously unthought-of location for the receiving line which will relieve congestion. Use a little imagination and ingenuity. (The bride does *not* have to receive in front of the fireplace—especially if that position might hamper "circulation.")

26. Ask caterer to telephone you for final number of guests.

27. Suggestion: Appoint or engage one person to be in the house on the wedding day to answer the phone, run errands, clean bathrooms when you leave for the church, and other odd chores.

EXTRA HELP

Name_____Phone_____

Name_____Phone_____

Name_____Phone_____

FLORIST

Name_____Phone_____

Address_____

1. Church decorations.

2. Reception decorations.

3. Decoration for wedding-cake table.

4. White satin ribbons and flowers for cake knife.

5. Small flowers tied with white ribbon on stems of champagne toast glasses.

6. Bride's bouquet. Discuss what will be suitable with her gown. Proportion is important. Some brides prefer to carry a white prayer book with or without flowers.

7. Bride's going-away corsage.

8. Corsages for bride's mother and groom's mother.

9. Boutonnieres for ushers, best man and groom.

10. Flowers for bride's attendants. Proportion, styling, and color are the important things—more desirable than a costly, poorly designed bouquet.

11. Time and place of delivery:

a. Bridal party_____(in time for photographs)

b. Mothers' corsages_____

_____

c. Ushers', best man's and groom's boutonnieres_____

d. Grandmothers' corsages_____

12. The florist can usually provide a canvas runner if such is desired for the aisle of the church.

NOTE: The groom customarily pays for the bride's bouquet, her going-away corsage, corsages for the mothers, boutonnieres for the ushers, best man and himself. He *may* pay for the attendants' flowers.

PHOTOGRAPHER

Name_____Phone_____

Address_____

1. Engage a photographer who is a specialist in weddings. An excellent portrait photographer is not necessarily adept at handling people discreetly. A specialist is familiar with wedding procedure, and he will anticipate the bridal couple's next move. He will be in the proper place at the proper time.

2. A clear understanding of what the photographer will do is essential. a. Ask your friends for their recommendations. b. Ask to see a photographer's finished work before you make a final decision. c. Get a firm price on pictures and albums. d. Decide whether you prefer black and white or color pictures. e. Make sure you can select the pictures that will make up the albums. f. Be sure you will have a sufficient number of proofs to allow an adequate selection. g. Make sure the photographer will take any special pictures you request. h. Make sure he will appear at the proper time and will stay through the reception.

3. Arrange a time and place for your formal portrait, if you desire one. Some gown salons provide space for this at the final fitting. Consider these advantages of having your portrait taken on the wedding day:
   1. The wedding bouquet will be your own.
   2. Your gown will not have to be transported to a studio.
   3. A bride *always* looks best on her wedding day.

31

4. Discuss what pictures you must have. Remember to ask for a picture of the groom's parents with the bride and groom —girl with the guest book—candids of certain relatives.

5. Arrange to have as many pictures as possible taken before the wedding: the bride with her bridesmaids; the bride with her father, her mother, her whole family.

6. Set the exact time for photographer to be at the church. Ascertain the church's rules regarding taking pictures. Some churches forbid it. If church pictures are allowed, remind the photographer to be discreet. Indicate that you do not want him to dash down the aisle in pursuit of a picture.

7. Instruct the photographer not to hold up the receiving line by taking too many pictures while guests are waiting. He has heard this many, many times. Tell him again.

8. Give him a list of newspapers which are to get wedding pictures.

9. Remind him that the best photographers are invisible.

MUSICIANS FOR THE CHURCH

Name_____Phone_____

Address_____

1. Make certain the musicians know or have music for special selections the bride or groom might request.

2. Arrange for a choir or soloist, if desired, for a very formal wedding.

3. Arrange to pay before or after the wedding day.

MUSICIANS FOR THE RECEPTION

Name_____Phone_____

Address_____

1. There need be no music at all at the reception. If you want music, however, it can be anything from a piano or an accordion to two dance bands.

2. Decide what the musicians will wear.

3. Set an exact time for the musicians' arrival at the reception.

4. Arrange for a special fanfare to announce the cake cutting, if you desire.

5. Give the leader a list of the bride's and groom's favorite selections for both background and dance music.

6. If there is to be no dancing, the musicians will play background music only.

7. If there is to be dancing, the musicians will play background music until the dancing begins. No one may dance until the bride and groom have had their first dance. The dancing sequence goes like this:

First dance: bride and groom alone.
Second dance: bride and her father; groom and bride's mother.

Third dance: bride and groom; bride's father and groom's mother; bride's mother and groom's father; ushers and bridesmaids. Then all dance. Anyone may cut in and dance with the bride. Guests love it.

DRIVERS

Bride to church, accompanied traditionally by her father (or father and mother):

DRIVER_____ PHONE_____

EXACT TIME TO BE AT HOUSE_____

Bridesmaids to church and return for the reception:

DRIVER_____ PHONE_____

DRIVER_____ PHONE_____

DRIVER_____ PHONE_____

DRIVER_____ PHONE_____

DRIVER_____ PHONE_____

Time to be at house_____

Bride's mother, unless she rides with bride or bridesmaids:

DRIVER_____ PHONE_____

Time to be at house_____

Groom's parents:

DRIVER_____ PHONE_____

TIME_____ PLACE_____

1. Have all been informed of the correct times and addresses?

2. Did you arrange for the groom's parents to return promptly from the church?

3. Bridesmaids may return from the church with the ushers—if they promise to return promptly.

4. If you hire drivers, arrange to pay them either before or after the wedding day.

INVITATIONS, ANNOUNCEMENTS AND ADDRESSING

If you appreciate the elegance of beautiful invitations, a reputable, established stationer is a great help. His well-trained people can advise you on the proper and popular styles of lettering, size and quality of paper, the correct wording for church or home weddings, and announcements. They are prepared to give you information on reception and ceremony cards and "at home" cards (which are enclosed in announcements only). They also understand the problems connected with divorced parents' invitations and are well qualified to help you—using the rules of etiquette, experience, and good taste. The very best stationery stores charge no more than stores that might not be satisfactory.

Order your invitations as soon as you can estimate your guest list. Close friends, even those living at great distance, consider it a compliment to receive an invitation. (If you feel that an invitation seems to call for a gift, you may prefer to send announcements to less intimate friends. This is your decision.)

Remember to include an address for responses, especially if the reception will not be held at your home.

Order extra envelopes to allow for mis-addressing. At the same time, order your announcements for later delivery. Before completing your order, consider this point: Traditionally, for a formal occasion, printed or glued-on sticker return addresses are not recommended. But a return address can be important. First choice—embossed in white on the envelope flap. You can order a die or, if you wish to economize, use an inexpensive home embosser. If you decide on the do-it-yourself plan, take the outside envelopes home and start addressing and squeezing your embosser. Professional addressers are available; perhaps your stationer can suggest one.

RULES FOR ADDRESSING

Now let's have some fun and play a game. Can you find nine mistakes in the following address?

> Mr. & Mrs. Chas. D. Blake and Family
> 33 E. 25th Ave.
> San Francisco
> Ca. 94112

You probably spotted them. If you did not, here are the rules for addressing.

1. Write "and." Symbols are not permissible.
2. "Charles," not "Chas." or "Wm."; write the name in full.
3. David, not "D." No initials are permissible. If you do not know what the initial stands for, omit it.
4. *Never* "and Family."
5. Write out "East" and "West," "North" and "South."
6. Write out "Twenty-fifth." Use no figures except for the house numbers and zip code.
7. Write out "Avenue." Also "Boulevard," "Road," and so on.
8. Spell out "California." Again, no abbreviation.
9. All invitations must be handwritten, preferably in permanent black ink. Never, never typewrite an address.

ADDRESSING INSTRUCTIONS

1. Place invitations in the inner, ungummed envelope. Folded invitations are inserted with the folded edge down. Envelope-sized invitations are inserted with the engraved side facing the back of the envelope.
2. Use your file cards and carefully address the envelopes.

Follow this guide:

A. To a husband and wife:

    Outer envelope: Mr. and Mrs. Joseph Guest
    Inner envelope: Mr. and Mrs. Guest

B. To a husband, wife, and children:

    Outer envelope: Mr. and Mrs. Joseph Guest
    Inner envelope: Mr. and Mrs. Guest
                  Elizabeth and John

C. To a single woman:

    Outer envelope: Miss Carolyn Guest
    Inner envelope: Miss Guest
This rule applies to girls of any age—no matter how young.

D. To a single man:

    Outer envelope: Mr. Thomas Guest
    Inner envelope: Mr. Guest
The title "Mr." is not used for very young boys; they may
be addressed as "Master."

E. To two sisters:

    Outer envelope: Misses (or, The Misses) Elizabeth and
        Mary Guest
    Inner envelope: Misses (or, The Misses) Guest

F. To two brothers:

    Outer envelope: Messrs. (or, The Messrs.) John and
        William Guest
    Inner envelope: Messrs. (or, The Messrs.) Guest

G. To a widow:

Outer envelope: Mrs. Robert Guest (never Mrs. Alice Guest)
Inner envelope: Mrs. Guest

H. To a divorcee:

Outer envelope: Mrs. Townsend Guest (her maiden name combined with her former husband's name—not Mrs. Barbara Guest or Mrs. Barbara Townsend Guest). See rule on page 43, item 6.

3. Address both the inner and outer envelopes in the same hand.

4. The inner envelope is inserted in the outer envelope upper side up so that the writing faces the back of the outer envelope.

5. Always send invitations and announcements sealed, first-class mail.

6. When addressing, sealing and stamping are completed, sort envelopes by destination. By mailing foreign or cross-country ones early, you avoid the cost of air mail. Invitations should be delivered approximately *four weeks before* the wedding.

7. Announcements are addressed in the same way as invitations.

8. Announcements should be mailed immediately *after* the wedding.

9. No announcements should be sent to those who received invitations.

10. Send a separate invitation to any person sixteen or older.

11. It is improper to write "No Children" on invitations. Here is one way to keep indulgent mothers from bringing uninvited children to the reception. Telephone them (after the invitations are sent) to suggest they may bring their children *to the church*. Explain that you are forced to limit the number of reception guests.

DIVORCED PARENTS

It is most important that divorced parents resolve to forget their differences and conceal personal feelings: The bride's feelings are the most important now. You will be admired if you handle the situation with dignity and co-operation. Circumstances vary widely, but here are a few possible guidelines for you:

INVITATIONS:

An experienced stationer will have suggestions and samples for you to see. Your own desire for harmony will guide you.

1. Invitations are often sent by the parent with whom the bride lives.

2. If the mother of the bride has remarried, she may send the invitations as "Mrs. New Husband's Name requests . . ." or, "Mr. and Mrs. New Husband's Name request . . . at the marriage of *her* daughter . . ." (giving the daughter's full name).

3. Sometimes the mother sends invitations to the wedding and the father sends invitations to the reception. He may give his daughter away at the altar. If he has remarried, his wife's name may appear with his on the reception invitations as host and hostess.

4. If the parents are separated but not legally divorced, they should ignore their differences and issue invitations under normal procedure.

5. Grandparents, brothers, or sisters may issue invitations if circumstances demand.

6. If the mother has not remarried and issues the invitations, she must use her correct divorced name. (If she was Miss Elizabeth Browning and married Mr. John Blake, from whom she is now divorced, her correct name is "Mrs. Browning Blake." It should appear that way on the invitations.)

SEATING IN CHURCH:

1. The mother of the bride sits in the first pew on the left. Her husband will be escorted to her pew early. If she has not remarried, she may sit alone or invite a close relative to sit with her. No casual escort, not even her intended husband, may sit with her. The head usher may escort her from the church.

2. After giving the bride away, her father sits in the second or third pew on the left with his parents or his wife if she attends.

3. The same seating arrangements apply for the groom's parents if they are divorced.

RECEIVING-LINE SUGGESTIONS:

1. Do not include the fathers—it is optional anyway.

2. If the bride's mother gives the reception, she stands in the line. The bride's father attends as a guest. If she has remarried, her husband does not stand in line; he acts as host.

3. Suggestions if the bride's father gives the reception: a. Remarried or not, he may relinquish his place in the line to the bride's mother—a happy solution. b. If he has not remarried, the bride's mother may stand in line either next to him or separated by the groom's parents. c. If he has remarried, he may stand first in the line. His wife does not stand in line; she acts as hostess. The bride's mother is a guest.

STATIONERY

These are the basic stationery requirements for your guidance:

1. Everyday paper for business letters and personal use. Handy to have printed name and address on single sheets.

2. Engraved calling cards and/or informals. Useful for invitations, responses, simple notes of thanks and to enclose with gifts.

3. Monogrammed note paper (see page 46).

4. Letter paper, monogrammed or plain. Plain stationery of good quality is preferable to fancy paper.

INITIALS AND MONOGRAMS

1. Towels and bed linens: Use the first initial of your first name, the initial of your maiden surname, and the first initial of your husband's surname—the latter being the largest or accentuated initial of the monogram.

2. Stationery: Same as above. For calling cards and informals, use Mr. and Mrs. and full name (no initials). Your address may also be engraved, but unless it is a permanent address, this may be an unnecessary extravagance.

3. Silver: Simple initial of your husband's surname is preferred. Second choice is the same as for stationery and linens. Silver is often passed down from one generation to another. If it is already monogrammed with initials other than your own, use it with pride.

4. Only for fun and informality on such as bar glasses would you combine your and your husband's first-name initials.

SIGNING YOUR NEW NAME

1. You will sign your name on checks and legal papers as given name, maiden name, husband's name: Barbara Townsend Long.

2. In letters to close friends, you will always be simply Barbara.

3. To friends who recognize your new name, you will sign Barbara Long—otherwise Barbara Townsend Long.

4. Business letters: Barbara Long
                        (Mrs. William Long)

LINENS

This list must be adapted to your own way of living and pocketbook. Therefore, the following list is simply a reminder. It can be enlarged or shortened. You will probably receive some linens as wedding or shower gifts.

For monogramming, see page 46.

CHECK LIST OF LINENS

1. Dining room:

Breakfast sets
Luncheon cloths, mats, and napkins
Informal dinner
Formal dinner
Buffet
Cocktail napkins
Bridge-table sets
Tray cloths
Doilies

2. Bedroom:

Sheets (six for each bed)
Pillowcases (four for each bed)
Blankets
Blanket covers
Mattress covers
Bedspread

3. Bathroom:

Bath towels
Hand towels
Washcloths
Bath mats
Guest towels

4. Kitchen:

Dish towels
Dishcloths
Cleaning cloths

SPECIAL PEW HOLDERS

1. Send reserved-pew cards to family members and very special friends you wish to honor. Request groom's parents to let you know how many they will need.

2. The bride's family sits on the left side of the church; the groom's family (as guests of honor) sit on the right.

3. It is better to send special pew cards *after* you receive acceptances. This way you avoid empty seats and the problem of re-arranging the seating plan.

4. Specially engraved cards for pew holders can be purchased from stationers. They are not often used. Usually the mother of the bride's calling cards or plain cards are used.

EXAMPLE:

Bride's reserved section. (To be written on calling card.)
   Pew No. 3
   Mrs. James Blue (as it is on calling card)
   Please present this card to usher. (To be written on card.)

I cannot sufficiently stress the importance of pew arrangements. Who wants fiery-tempered relatives on this special day?

Bride's (left) side:

NAME_____PEW_____

NAME_____PEW_____

NAME_____PEW_____

NAME_____PEW_____

NAME_____PEW_____

NAME_____PEW_____

NAME_____PEW_____

NAME_____PEW_____

NAME_____PEW_____

Groom's (right) side:

NAME_____PEW_____

NAME_____PEW_____

NAME_____PEW_____

NAME_____PEW_____

NAME_____PEW_____

NAME_____PEW_____

NAME_____PEW_____

NAME_____PEW_____

NAME_____PEW_____

5. Go over this list with the head usher. Be sure he understands all arrangements.

6. Give a list of all special-pew holders to each usher, in case guests have forgotten their pew cards.

DISPLAYING YOUR GIFTS

Part of the fun of a home wedding reception is seeing the gifts of the bridal couple.

A simple white cloth can be used to cover the table. Or you might prefer to use a white satin cloth. Ribbon bows or artificial sprays of white flowers are very pretty. You might even have your florist do a professional display table for you —if you are in an extravagant mood. If the reception is held away from your home, do not take gifts to display.

Gift-display tips:

1. Do not exhibit cards of donors.

2. Do not display checks. (An empty envelope or a card bearing the word "check" may be placed on the table.)

3. Arrange the gifts as artistically as possible.

4. Separate similar gifts.

5. If exact duplicates have been received, display only one. Each donor will be happier. It might be that the identical gifts make a handsome pair: in that case, display them both.

6. You may be able to borrow plate-and-tray display racks from a gift shop.

7. When displaying dinnerware, crystal and silver, use only one place setting.

8. Gifts should be exchanged *after* the wedding. With the exceptions noted above, all gifts should be displayed.

9. Appoint someone to be in charge of gifts which guests occasionally bring to the reception. It is not proper to open them at that time.

THE WEDDING REHEARSAL

This is a pleasant and important part of the wedding routine, especially if it follows, or is to be followed by, a rehearsal dinner for the bridal party, their wives, husbands, fiancés, and both sets of parents.

All members of the wedding party and the clergyman and organist should be present at the church. At that time the clergyman will give you complete directions about everything—the processional, the ceremony, and the recessional.

NOTE: I have deliberately omitted descriptions of various religious rituals. You are concerned only with your own, and the necessary details have been discussed in an earlier conference with your clergyman.

Most brides today ignore the old superstition that required the maid or matron of honor to stand in for them during the rehearsal, but it is up to you. Whether or not you take an active part in the rehearsal, there are a few decisions that only you can make.

1. If you have both a matron of honor and a maid of honor, you must decide which will hold your bouquet during the ceremony. You must also decide who will hold the groom's ring, if you are having a double-ring ceremony.

2. You may have a preference as to the step you and your bridesmaids will use in the processional. The "hesitation step" is not as popular as it once was. I suggest the more natural, slow walk. It is easier and more graceful.

3. Most frequently in the recessional, the ushers and the bridesmaids are paired. If their numbers are unequal, plan to have the bridesmaids walk first, followed by the ushers.

4. If this is the ushers' first experience, remind them to ask guests, "Friends of the bride or groom?" Friends of the bride are seated on the left; friends of the groom on the right. (If one family is represented by very few guests, you may ask the ushers to seat the guests indiscriminately.)

5. Now is the time, while you are at the church, to make sure the ushers understand about the reserved pews.

6. Instruct the ushers that when it is time for the ceremony to begin the grandparents should be escorted to their pews. Next, the head usher will escort the groom's mother to the first pew on the right. If her son is an usher he should do the honors. Her husband will follow a step or two behind them.

7. A reminder: The mother of the bride is the last person to enter the church escorted by the head usher or her son, if he is an usher. No one may be seated after her. She is the first to stand when the wedding procession begins. The guests follow her lead.

8. Which arm? Should you take your father's left or right arm? Take whichever you wish—there is no rule. But decide at the rehearsal. If you take your father's right arm, he can reach his pew more easily, especially if your train is long. Also this will put you nearer the groom's side of the church walking down the aisle and closer to your own friends and relatives in the recessional, when you will be on your groom's right arm.

9. Decide whether you wish your maid of honor or the groom to fold back your veil at the altar.

THE RECEPTION

If there is to be no reception, the receiving line quickly forms in the vestibule of the church. The wedding party and the mothers take the same position as shown below. In this case, fathers do not stand in the receiving line.

A wedding reception, like any other form of entertaining, should be planned with your guests' enjoyment in mind. Because you want them to be as happy as you are, you must be extravagant in your planning. Ask the photographer to be as speedy as possible when he takes pictures of the receiving line. Recall that the waiting guests can sometimes be cheered with glasses of champagne. Because you, the bride, and your mother, will not be free to circulate among your guests until your receiving-line duties are done, alert close friends or relatives to watch out for specific out-of-town guests who might be standing alone. (Here, a professional hostess can be a comfort.)

RECEIVING LINE POSITIONS AND PROCEDURES

1. Mother of the bride
2. Father of the groom (optional)
3. Mother of the groom
4. Father of the bride (optional)
5. Bride
6. Groom
7. Maid or matron of honor
8. Bridesmaids

Ushers and the best man—unless he is also the father—do *not* stand in the receiving line.

Frequently fathers are not in line but are close by to greet their friends.

If the bride has no mother, her father or a close relative may be at the head of the line.

Mothers should wear their gloves while receiving.

An announcer who asks the name of each guest and relays it to the mother of the bride is sometimes used for very formal weddings. Usually, however, a considerate guest will quickly give his name to jog your memory.

When your guests reach the receiving line, they plan to say only a few words of congratulations and admiration. Greet each person cordially. Let him know you are happy he is there. Then, quickly and graciously, introduce him to the next in line. By taking only a few moments, you will be doing all your guests a favor.

GIFT-DISPLAY TABLE

You might arrange to divert some of your guests by having them shown to the gift display while they are waiting to reach the receiving line.

TYPES OF MENUS

This depends on the time of day.

THE WEDDING BREAKFAST

The "breakfast" is, in fact, lunch. It takes place after a morning or noon ceremony and may be served at tables or from a buffet.

AFTERNOON RECEPTION

A tea or cocktail menu is served, with the addition of the wedding cake. A late-afternoon reception may be prolonged until a dinner or supper is served, either at tables or from a buffet. If you plan to serve dinner, be sure the reception invitations say so.

EVENING RECEPTION

Similar to the afternoon reception. Frequently a late supper is served, especially if guests stay for dancing.

THE BRIDE'S TABLE

Even if the guests serve themselves from a buffet, it is acceptable to have a bride's table at a large, formal wedding. This table is usually for the wedding party only—without husbands, wives, fiancés, or parents. Parents may have a separate table, if they wish, along with the groom's parents as guests of honor, and including grandparents, close friends, and the clergyman and his wife. The party at the bride's table is served at the table. More frequently, unless all the guests are seated, there is no bride's table and the bride and groom move freely among the guests.

DANCING

When the bride and groom are ready for their first dance, the orchestra swings into their favorite dance tune. (See page 34 for order of the dances.)

TOASTING THE BRIDE

The best man offers the first toast to the bride. If there is no bride's table, he will most usually toast the bride at the wedding-cake table, before the cake is cut. Other toasts may then be offered by the groom and the fathers of the bride and groom. The bride and groom drink to one another. After the toast, the best man will read a few congratulatory telegrams.

CUTTING THE CAKE

The bride uses a knife decorated with ribbons or flowers. She cuts the first slice from the lowest layer of the cake and shares it with the groom, feeding him the first bite. Bite—not an entire slice.

THROWING THE BOUQUET

Before leaving to change to her going-away clothes, the bride, with the groom at her side, tosses her bouquet to her bridesmaids. Sometimes other unmarried girls gather to try to catch the significant "next-to-be-married" symbol. It is best to try to keep very young girls away so the eligible young ladies can have a fair chance at the bouquet—unless you especially want to honor a younger sister. Throw the bouquet from a stairway, an upstairs window, or a balcony; a small raised platform covered in white is also suitable. Many brides throw a bridal garter to the bachelors as a "next-to-be-married" symbol.

CHANGING TO GOING-AWAY CLOTHES

The maid of honor accompanies the bride to help her change. Bridesmaids may follow. Ushers accompany the groom. Just before the bride and groom are ready to leave, the maid of honor notifies the parents of the bride and groom so they can have a short, private good-by.

LEAVING THE RECEPTION

While you are changing, rose petals, confetti, or rice will be passed to the guests. (Rice can sting faces and make stairs slippery; rose petals can stain rugs. Artificial rose petals are usually available.) The best man will drive the getaway car or see that the one he ordered is ready. The final dash for the car can be a happy and memorable moment for you and the guests.

FOR THE GROOM

The groom has fewer details to worry about than the bride, but he has certain responsibilities. Here is his special check list:

1. Beat the deadline for turning in your guest list and your family's guest list. You will endear yourself to your future mother-in-law.
2. Arrange your business affairs:
   Draw a will.
   Change the beneficiary on your life insurance.
   Arrange a joint bank account or a separate account for your bride.
3. Purchase a wedding ring for the bride.
4. Purchase a gift for the bride.
5. Purchase a permanent keepsake for each of the ushers. The best man's gift may be a similar article but a bit more expensive. These may be given at the bachelor dinner or the rehearsal party.
6. Make arrangements for the honeymoon. (You pay for the honeymoon.)
7. Get a physical checkup. Get a dental checkup. Get your blood test.
8. Make financial arrangements for home or apartment and utilities.
9. Arrange for a conference with the clergyman; both you and the bride should be present.
10. Go with your bride to get the marriage license.
11. Do not put off your haircut until just before the wedding. Avoid that new-shorn look.

12. Decide what you and the ushers will wear—in keeping with the kind of wedding your bride has planned. The bride's father and your father should wear the same type of suits as you and the ushers. (Tuxedos should not be worn before six in the evening.)

13. Blacken the soles of your shoes. They will look better when you kneel at the altar.

14. You pay the clergyman's fee. Put it in an envelope (new currency, from ten dollars to two hundred dollars) and give it to your best man. He will give it to the clergyman in the vestry room either before or after the ceremony.

15. Arrange to be billed by the florist who is making the wedding bouquets. You will be expected to pay for the bride's bouquet, her going-away corsage, corsages for the mothers, and the boutonnieres for yourself and the ushers. All these will be ordered by the bride or her mother. Bridesmaids' bouquets may be purchased by you, or may be considered part of the *décor*.

16. The bachelor dinner is usually arranged by the best man. It may be given by you or by your ushers. Try to have it early in the week before the wedding.

17. Be of good cheer.

MEN'S ATTIRE

Selection of the men's clothes depends on the degree of formality of the wedding, the bride's gown, the time of day and the season of the year.

1. For a formal wedding in the daytime: Oxford gray cutaway coat, striped gray or black trousers, lighter gray waistcoat. A starched winged collar with an ascot or a starched plain collar with a four-in-hand tie. Gray doeskin gloves. Plain-toed black shoes and black socks.

2. For a semi-formal daytime wedding: Short Oxford gray director's coat, double-breasted gray waistcoat, four-in-hand tie. Gray doeskin gloves; plain black shoes and black socks.

3. For an informal daytime wedding: Oxford gray or dark blue suit, four-in-hand tie, black shoes and socks. At a summer wedding in the country or suburbs, the men may wear suits appropriate to the occasion.

4. For a formal wedding in the evening, all seasons: Tailcoat, white piqué waistcoat, stiff-bosomed shirt with starched wing collar and white bow tie. Black dress pumps and black socks. White kid gloves.

5. For a semi-formal wedding in the evening: Black or midnight blue dinner jacket, black or midnight blue vest or cummerbund and matching bow tie. Dress shirt. Black, plain-toed shoes or dress pumps. Black socks. In summer, white or colored dinner jackets may be worn.

The groom, best man, ushers, and both fathers wear the same kind of suits. The ushers' ascots or four-in-hands should all be alike but they may be different from the groom's and best man's. The same choice applies to their boutonnieres—the groom and best man may wear lilies of the valley, while the ushers wear white carnations. Shirts are white in every case.

NOTE: It is customary for the groom to give appropriate ties and gloves to the best man and ushers.

USHERS' DUTIES

1. Ushers pay for their own outfits. If you rent, have an early fitting to allow time for adjustments.

2. Attend the wedding rehearsal. On time.

3. On the wedding day, arrive at the church an hour ahead of time.

4. Pin your boutonniere to your left lapel. Forget the buttonhole; it is only decorative.

5. Offer your *right* arm to each feminine guest and escort her to a pew. Ask if she is a friend of the bride or groom. Bride's friends sit on the left of the aisle; groom's on the right. As the church fills, it may be necessary to balance off the guests on either side of the aisle. When you escort a lady, the men and children in her group will follow you to the pew. The same procedure is followed with unaccompanied men, but you do not offer your arm.

6. The *head usher* seats the mother of the groom. Her husband follows a few steps behind. The *head usher* escorts the mother of the bride to her pew. She is the last person to be seated. If her son is an usher, he may escort his mother if she prefers.

7. At a very formal wedding, a white runner, furnished by the florist, may be laid on the center aisle. If the runner is in place before the guests arrive, they are shown to their pews from side aisles. At other times, the runner is placed by two ushers after the mother of the bride is seated.

8. Familiarize yourself with the special pew-holders' seating plan.

9. In churches where there is a balcony, an extra usher may be assigned to seat guests there. Since late-arriving guests will probably be seated in the balcony, it is not necessary for this extra usher to be in the processional.

10. Two or more ushers may be asked to return after the recessional to escort the bride's and groom's mothers and grandmothers out of the church. More often the bride's mother and father lead the way, followed by the groom's parents, and the guests follow, alternating left and right, row by row.

11. The ushers are responsible for transporting the bridesmaids from the church to the reception. Promptly.

12. Ushers, as a group, give the groom a memento. A popular gift is a silver box with your signatures engraved on the lid. Your wedding gift to the bride may be given by the entire group of ushers or individually.

13. At very large receptions, an announcer is sometimes hired to give guests' names quietly to the first person in the receiving line. A more informal way to jog memories: ask ushers to take turns announcing the guests.

14. In the festivities immediately preceding the wedding, unmarried ushers are expected to escort bridesmaids to parties—regardless of personal whim.

15. Practical jokes can be funny as long as they do not interfere with the solemnity of the wedding or endanger the safety of the wedding party and guests.

BRIDESMAIDS' DUTIES

The bridesmaids have few duties. It is their function to add gaiety and beauty and a warm feeling to the wedding and reception. (Nothing goes further than a happy, relaxed smile as they walk down the aisle of the church—this is a joyous occasion and they should show their joy.) Their presence assures the bride that she is surrounded by close friends on her great day.

Often bridesmaids plan showers or other parties for the bride.

They should co-operate by having their gowns and shoes fitted promptly and in meeting their social obligations during the prenuptial party time.

MAID OF HONOR (OR MATRON OF HONOR)

1. You *do* have more to do than the other attendants. You help the bride dress on her wedding day.

2. You hold her bouquet, and possibly her gloves, during the ceremony.

3. If it is a double-ring ceremony, you hold the groom's ring.

4. If the bride wishes, you may fold back her veil at the altar.

5. You help the bride change from her wedding gown to her going-away outfit.

6. It is your duty to inform the parents of the bride and groom when the newlyweds are ready to leave.

7. You stand in the receiving line with the other attendants. You can help speed up the line by introducing the next bridesmaid clearly and with pleasure.

8. After the receiving line dissolves, mingle with the guests and have fun.

9. You are an extra pair of legs and an extra head for the bride on her exciting day. You can help smooth her way.

FLOWER GIRL AND RING BEARER

1. The ring bearer should wear his best dress-up suit. Navy blue or, perhaps, white linen in the summer.

2. He carries a white satin pillow with the wedding ring (the real one or a substitute) stitched on.

3. The flower girl's dress should harmonize with the bridesmaids' gowns. Her bouquet should be scaled down in size.

4. Instead of a bouquet, the flower girl may carry a basket of paper rose petals to strew along the bride's path.

5. If the wedding procession includes both a ring bearer and a flower girl, they precede the bride and her escort in that order. In the recessional, they follow the bride and groom and walk side by side.

6. Parents of the children pay for their wedding-party clothes.

7. Include the flower girl, the ring bearer, and their parents in your arrangements for transportation.

8. The children probably will be too young to join the receiving line.

9. Give each child a keepsake gift and a photograph of the wedding party.

10. Invite their parents to substitute for them at the rehearsal dinner.

NOTE: A junior bridesmaid has the same duties and privileges as the other bridesmaids. Her gown may be modified to suit her age. She walks first in the wedding procession unless, as the bride's sister, she is the maid of honor.

THE GROOM'S PARENTS

Because almost all wedding responsibilities and decisions belong to the bride and her parents, a groom's family may feel superfluous—even the groom feels forgotten at moments during the hectic rush of bridal activities. But, did you ever hear of a groom-less wedding? Never! He is essential and so are you as his parents.

You will play an important role as special guests of honor. Read this entire book in order to understand and sympathize with all the bride must do—then follow this chapter for your own list of Do's and Don'ts. You will feel at ease if you know exactly what you should do.

THE ENGAGEMENT

As soon as your son tells you, "She said yes," telephone the bride-to-be to express your pleasure that she is going to be your new daughter. Next, telephone her parents and arrange to call on them. Talk about the bride. Your interest in her can contribute both to your son's happiness and your share in it. If her parents live out of town write them an enthusiastic letter.

After the engagement announcement, you might like to give a tea or cocktail party to introduce the bride to your friends. If not, you may entertain for her or for both of them after their wedding trip.

When you plan a party, remember that a shower hosted by a member of either family is taboo.

If you live nearby, you will be invited to showers for the bride. Take a gift. If you live out of town you might receive courtesy shower invitations. If possible, send the bride a gift in care of the shower hostess.

The groom's obligations are listed on pages 61 and 62. If he is still a student, no doubt you will assist him.

Give the bridal couple a present. Suggestions: silver, a family heirloom, a more extensive honeymoon trip than the groom can afford, furniture for their new home, a check.

Give the bride a personal gift—perhaps a piece of jewelry.

You have no financial responsibilities for the wedding. If you wonder if you may assist financially to make the wedding more elaborate than the bride's family can afford, read page x of the Introduction. It explains why you may not.

Rare exceptions may occur. For example, if the bride is an orphan with no other relatives to take over, or if her parents live in a foreign country or too distant city, then you may offer to give the wedding.

If you host the wedding the invitations should be worded:

> Mr. and Mrs. Your Name
> request the honour of your presence
> at the marriage of
> Miss Bride's Name
> to their son
> Mr. Groom's Name . . . etc.

This is the correct form for a church wedding. A home wedding invitation would read, "Requests the pleasure of your company."

Note in the example an unusual case when "Miss" is correct.

GENERAL PLANS

Co-operation is the keynote. Co-operate with all the bride's decisions but do not attempt to make any.

1. Limit your guest list to the number of places the bride's parents allot you. They may be restricted by space or budget limitations.
2. Submit your guest list on or ahead of schedule. Important!
3. Spare the bride the tedious task of organizing your list. Make a separate file card with each guest's full name and address. Follow the form shown on page 1 of this book. Use the same procedure for your announcement list provided announcements are to be ordered.
4. Offer to help address invitations but do not be offended if the bride prefers to do it herself.
5. Even though you might prefer another style or period of china, silver or furniture, remember that the young couple must feel free to carry out their own tastes without outside pressure.
6. Occasionally a groom invites his father to serve as best man. Don't feel disappointed if your son chooses a close friend. Co-operate with his decisions, too.

WHAT TO WEAR

The bride's mother will select her outfit first, then expect you to co-operate with the effect she and the bride are trying to achieve. Refer to page 9, item 37. If you are not enthusiastic, take heart. When your daughter marries, *you* will have first choice.

The groom's father should dress in the same type of suit as the other men in the wedding party.

REHEARSAL PARTY

The groom's parents frequently offer to give this party—usually a dinner preceding or following the rehearsal. This will be your one opportunity to contribute to an important pre-wedding affair. Besides, you will have fun.

1. *Where to hold the party*

Give the party wherever convenient—at home, in a club, hotel or restaurant.

Even if your dinner will take place in a city where you are strangers you can make advance arrangements. Consult the bride's parents for their recommendations, then arrange details by direct correspondence with the hotel or restaurant.

2. *What to check*

Ask the catering department to submit:
- —Several detailed menus from which to choose
- —Wine list
- —Complete prices

Specify:
- —Private dining room
- —Desired arrangement of tables such as T or U shape
- —Table appointments such as candles and linens
- —When you order flowers agree on exactly what you want and the cost because prices vary startlingly in different sections of the country. You need not confine the decorations to white—any timely, romantic or colorful theme is appropriate.

3. *Whom to invite*

Consult the bride for her list. In addition to the members of the wedding party, expect to include the attendants' husbands, wives and fiancés and—*if* the bride wishes—those special relatives and friends who will travel some distance to the wedding.

The clergyman and his wife are invited only if they are close friends of either family.

4. *How to invite*

Even though you are certain everyone knows about the rehearsal party plans, send written invitations. This will avoid confusion about the time and place, and the possibility of overlooking a guest.

5. *At the dinner*

Your party will be more successful if you arrange the seating in advance to take care of the different age groups and those who might find themselves strangers.

If the party is given away from home, arrive well ahead of time to arrange place cards, check the tables, and be ready to greet your guests.

6. *A toast to the bride*

The groom's father should be prepared to give a toast. He may mention his new family-to-be but his main words should be directed to the bride.

7. *What about music and dancing?*

Make the party as simple or as elaborate as you wish. If you decide on music, plan it for only a short time. Rehearsal dinners usually break up early if they are held on the night before the wedding.

IN CHURCH

And now for the proud moment!

The bride's mother is the last person seated before the processional starts. The groom's mother is the next to last.

The head usher will escort you or, if you have another son who is a member of the wedding party (other than best man), ask that he accompany you.

The groom's father will follow a step or two behind.

You will sit in the first pew on the right-hand side—father in the aisle seat.

If your relatives attend the wedding be certain that pews are reserved for them and that they identify themselves to the ushers. Refer to page 50 for important procedures.

Leave the church immediately after the recessional. The receiving line cannot start until you take your place in it.

Now the solemnities are over and it is almost time to relax. Your last official duty is to stand in the receiving line and do your part to keep it moving smoothly. Don't hold up the line by chatting at length with your own friends but introduce them promptly to the next person in line. When the line disbands you will be free to chat.

Sometimes the fathers stand in the receiving line. This decision is made by the bride. Refer to page 57.

Mothers usually keep their gloves on but if the bride's mother removes hers, follow her lead.

When it is time for the bride and groom to leave on their honeymoon one of their attendants will take you to them for a quick hug and a kiss.

And then—give a silent toast to their enduring future happiness.

AFTER THE WEDDING

After the bride and groom leave, you, the mother of the bride will still have tasks. You will probably welcome them; you may feel the need to keep busy after the departure of your daughter.

1. You must plan to entertain out-of-town guests. Perhaps a supper for them, members of the wedding party, and close relatives can be planned after an afternoon wedding.

2. If the top layer of the wedding cake was fruitcake, wrap it well so it will keep for the bride and groom's first anniversary.

3. Mail the announcements of the marriage the day after the wedding, unless a friend has been charged with this duty.

4. Answer telegrams sent to you. Keep the telegrams sent to the bride and groom for them to acknowledge later.

5. Have wedding gown cleaned and professionally preserved in an airtight container to keep it from yellowing.

6. If you will send handwritten acknowledgment cards to those whose gifts arrived late, the gesture will be much appreciated.

EXAMPLE:

> "Your beautiful gift (or bowl or tray or what-
> ever) was received. Sue will write to you personally
> after she and Tom return from their wedding trip."

7. It is a nice gesture to write thank-you notes to the society
   editors of the papers you have been dealing with. You will
   be the exception, but they will love you for it.

THE NON-TRADITIONAL WEDDING

If you are one of today's brides who wants to break with tradition, this section is for you.

Because you want your wedding to express your own ideas, *all the more reason to make it perfect*.

Even the most informal-appearing affair cannot happen by itself. For any style of festivity or ceremony, you must decide exactly what you want, then carry it out step by step, carefully, completely, and consistently.

These two words say it all—*consistency* and *completeness*.

As I said in the "Introduction," not every item will apply to every wedding. But many of the preceding details and reminders need to be considered whether the wedding is to take place in a church or a barn, a garden or a hilltop, at the shore of the sea or under the sea.

So read all that has gone before and use whatever applies to your plans; then note the few extra and special reminders for unconventional situations.

SELECTING A LOCATION

If your special dream setting is a mountain peak, a forest, a meadow, a sea or lake shore—any isolated out-of-doors location—you need to think of these things.

1. A reasonably accessible site.
2. Adequate off-the-road parking.

3. In case of rain, an alternative roofed location nearby. A barn? A hall? A cabin? And a few umbrellas in the trunk of the car.

4. Privacy. A location least likely to be interrupted by the sounds of picnickers or hikers during the ceremony. Could you be lucky enough to know the owner of private waterfront or wooded property who might let you use it for the occasion?

5. If you select a public park, check to see if you can and should reserve it.

6. A caution: Sounds do not carry well out of doors. Plan to speak distinctly during the ceremony.

WHO WILL OFFICIATE

Keep in mind that you and your husband-to-be will marry one another, and that a minister, rabbi, priest, judge or other official will simply officiate at your marriage.

You will find that individual clergymen often vary in their attitudes toward self-written vows and other changes in church ritual. Because of these varying attitudes, you need to consult with the "officiator" of your choice early.

1. Discuss with utmost frankness your desires, plans and innovations.

2. Find out if he will agree to any extra demands upon him. (Need he fly in a plane . . . mount a horse . . . sail in a boat?)

3. Tell him how much additional time he will need to perform the ceremony away from his church.

4. If you wish two clergymen, each of a different faith, to officiate jointly, consult with each one to complete the necessary arrangements.

5. Will you need to provide a kneeling cushion? A raised platform as a focal point?

HOW TO INVITE

When you shop for invitations, you will find an almost limitless and overwhelming number of choices of color, size, design and wording. This gives you the opportunity to express your individuality or carry out a theme. Some invitations which introduce color or a beautifully executed design are similar to fine stationery.

Some additions:

1. Include explicit directions and a map if you have chosen a hard-to-find location.

2. If it is to be an outdoor location, specify where to meet in case of rain.

3. For the non-traditional wedding, occasionally the bride's and groom's parents will issue a joint invitation.

TRANSPORTATION

The bride's responsibility to arrange transportation for the bridal party to and from the wedding becomes even more urgent if the location is hard to find. Include the groom's parents in your arrangements, especially if they are from out of town.

NOTE: Furnish each driver with a map or explicit directions—with an estimate of the time needed to reach his destination.

WHAT TO WEAR

What is the picture you wish to create? Pastoral? Medieval? Casual? If you will dress to complete that picture all will be perfect.

—Rich, bright tones are a throwback to the Middle Ages when most brides wore brightly colored gowns trimmed with braid or jewels for their summer outdoor weddings.

—A satin cathedral train among the thistles? Inconsistent, wouldn't you say?

—Headdress. Whatever harmonizes with your dress and the setting. A few ideas:

1. If out of doors, a short, fluffy, soft veil is pretty.
2. A picture hat.
3. Harmonizing "costume" headdress.
4. Flowers or leaves—using varieties that will not wilt too soon.
5. Ribbons entwined in your hair.
6. No head covering at all.
7. No matter which, your hairdo should be consistent with your outfit, not a showpiece in itself.

—Bare feet? Yes, if they add to the total look. No, if it might appear that you forgot your shoes.

—If you will be far from "civilization," add first-aid items to your emergency kit.

—Talk over with your husband-to-be what he and the other men will wear—and agree on the over-all look you want to present.

FLOWERS AND DECORATIONS

Continue with your own ideas about the look of your wedding—the total effect. A few thoughts:

1. Preferable to hothouse blooms for an outdoor wedding are:

—varieties of garden flowers.
—baskets of field flowers if you can use them before they wilt.
—a single flower.

—sheaves of golden wheat. They can add a rich note. Be forewarned that in Elizabethan times they signified fertility.

2. In a natural setting you will usually need little or no decoration except for the buffet table.

3. If you need to transport flowers some distance, be sure to select long-lasting varieties.
   —To prolong their lives, harden them as follows: Submerge the stems in a container of water and cut them under water to prevent air pockets from forming. Soak for several hours or overnight.
   —Transport them in tip-proof containers.

WHAT TO SERVE AT YOUR RECEPTION

Although this subject has been fully check-listed in the preceding pages, a few additional ideas for special cases follow.

1. Unless the site of the ceremony is also ideal for your reception, plan to serve refreshments elsewhere—your home, a friend's home, rented or public quarters.

2. Portable refrigeration equipment. If you are engaging a caterer, be certain he can provide it. If you are arranging the reception yourself (or with the help of friends and family), try to obtain coolers for the wine, other beverages and food—even inexpensive Styrofoam containers.

3. The menu. Plan on "finger food" for ease in serving. If food must go unrefrigerated for any length of time, avoid mayonnaise, cream sauces or custard fillings.

4. The cake. A sugar frosting keeps well whereas a cream frosting might spoil.

5. Keep in mind that if you are far from home there will be no nearby kitchen for your last-minute needs. Now is the time to think, plan, check previous chapters and lists so you

can pack everything in advance. In addition, will you need any of the following?

—Folding tables and chairs.
—Cushions or a plastic tarpaulin.
—Easy-to-pack plastic wine glasses.

MUSIC

Music helps to create and complete the mood you want —pastoral or solemn or festive. Choose your favorite instruments and your favorite selections. Some considerations:

—Among the easily portable instruments are guitars, violins, flutes.
—A small organ can be transported with a little more trouble.
—If you want your guests to join in the singing or responsive reading, arrange to have copies of their "script" distributed.
—Do you want background music, music to dance by, or both?
—Don't hesitate to accept the offer of talented musical friends if they want to be a part of your wedding festivities as instrumentalists or singers. You can send them a thank-you gift and a photo or two of themselves at the wedding.

PICTURES

If you do not have photographs taken on your special day you will always regret it. A competent friend may be able to "cover" your wedding. Remember to provide him with plenty of film. Even if he is donating his services, talk over the not-to-be missed pictures with him. After the wedding, send him a gift as a thank-you for a difficult job well done.

ITEM

Ecology-minded brides furnish their guests with birdseed in place of traditional rice or rose petals. A combination self-clean product and bird feeder.

A FINAL THOUGHT

All my admonitions and lists are for one purpose—to help you have a perfect wedding. Whether you followed the traditions or your own ideas, you can be confident all has been done—everything possible for your start in life.

Happy wedding,
Happy life.

USE THESE CALENDAR PAGES
TO KEEP A RECORD
OF ALL YOUR APPOINTMENTS

The wedding date is _____.
              (month)   (date)

This week of _____ is the eleventh week
              (month)   (date)
before the wedding.

	Morning	Afternoon	Evening
SUNDAY			
MONDAY			
TUESDAY			
WEDNESDAY			
THURSDAY			
FRIDAY			
SATURDAY			

The wedding date is _____.
                        (month)   (date)

This week of _____ is the tenth week
                (month)   (date)
before the wedding.

	Morning	Afternoon	Evening
SUNDAY			
MONDAY			
TUESDAY			
WEDNESDAY			
THURSDAY			
FRIDAY			
SATURDAY			

The wedding date is _____.
                             (month)   (date)

This week of _____ is the ninth week
             (month)   (date)
before the wedding.

	Morning	*Afternoon*	*Evening*
SUNDAY			
MONDAY			
TUESDAY			
WEDNESDAY			
THURSDAY			
FRIDAY			
SATURDAY			

The wedding date is _____.
                 (month)   (date)

This week of _____ is the eighth week
          (month)   (date)
before the wedding.

	Morning	Afternoon	Evening
SUNDAY			
MONDAY			
TUESDAY			
WEDNESDAY			
THURSDAY			
FRIDAY			
SATURDAY			

The wedding date is _____.
                         (month)   (date)

This week of _____ is the seventh week
             (month)   (date)

before the wedding.

	Morning	Afternoon	Evening
SUNDAY			
MONDAY			
TUESDAY			
WEDNESDAY			
THURSDAY			
FRIDAY			
SATURDAY			

The wedding date is _June 5th_
                   (month)   (date)
This week of _April 26th_ is the sixth week
            (month)   (date)
before the wedding.

	Morning	Afternoon	Evening
SUNDAY			
MONDAY			
TUESDAY			
WEDNESDAY			
THURSDAY			
FRIDAY			
SATURDAY			

The wedding date is _____.
                        (month)   (date)

This week of _____ is the fifth week
                (month)   (date)
before the wedding.

	Morning	Afternoon	Evening
SUNDAY			
MONDAY			
TUESDAY			
WEDNESDAY			
THURSDAY			
FRIDAY			
SATURDAY			

The wedding date is _____,
                         (month)   (date)

This week of _____ is the fourth week
               (month)   (date)

before the wedding.

	Morning	Afternoon	Evening
SUNDAY			
MONDAY			
TUESDAY			
WEDNESDAY			
THURSDAY			
FRIDAY			
SATURDAY			

The wedding date is _____
                        (month)   (date)

This week of _____ is the third week
              (month)   (date)
before the wedding.

	Morning	Afternoon	Evening
SUNDAY			
MONDAY			
TUESDAY			
WEDNESDAY			
THURSDAY			
FRIDAY			
SATURDAY			

The wedding date is _____
                    (month)   (date)

This week of _____ is the second week
              (month)   (date)
before the wedding.

	Morning	*Afternoon*	*Evening*
SUNDAY			
MONDAY			
TUESDAY			
WEDNESDAY			
THURSDAY			
FRIDAY			
SATURDAY			

The wedding date is _____.
                      (month)   (date)

This week of _____ is the week before
             (month)   (date)
the wedding.

	Morning	Afternoon	Evening
SUNDAY			
MONDAY			
TUESDAY			
WEDNESDAY			
THURSDAY			
FRIDAY			
SATURDAY			

The wedding date is _____.
                       (month)   (date)

This week of _____ is the week of
          (month)   (date)

the wedding.

	Morning	Afternoon	Evening
SUNDAY			
MONDAY			
TUESDAY			
WEDNESDAY			
THURSDAY			
FRIDAY			
SATURDAY			

NOTES

NOTES

NOTES

NOTES

NOTES

NOTES

NOTES

NOTES

NOTES

NOTES

NOTES

CAKE

MENU

GUEST LISTS

FLORIST

RECEPTION MUSIC

TRANSPORTATION

FITTINGS (WEDDING)
                   PARTY

#26

TROUSSEAU

APT

NOTES

NOTES

NOTES

NOTES